NG SCIENCE PROJECTS

PLANTS

Sally Hewitt

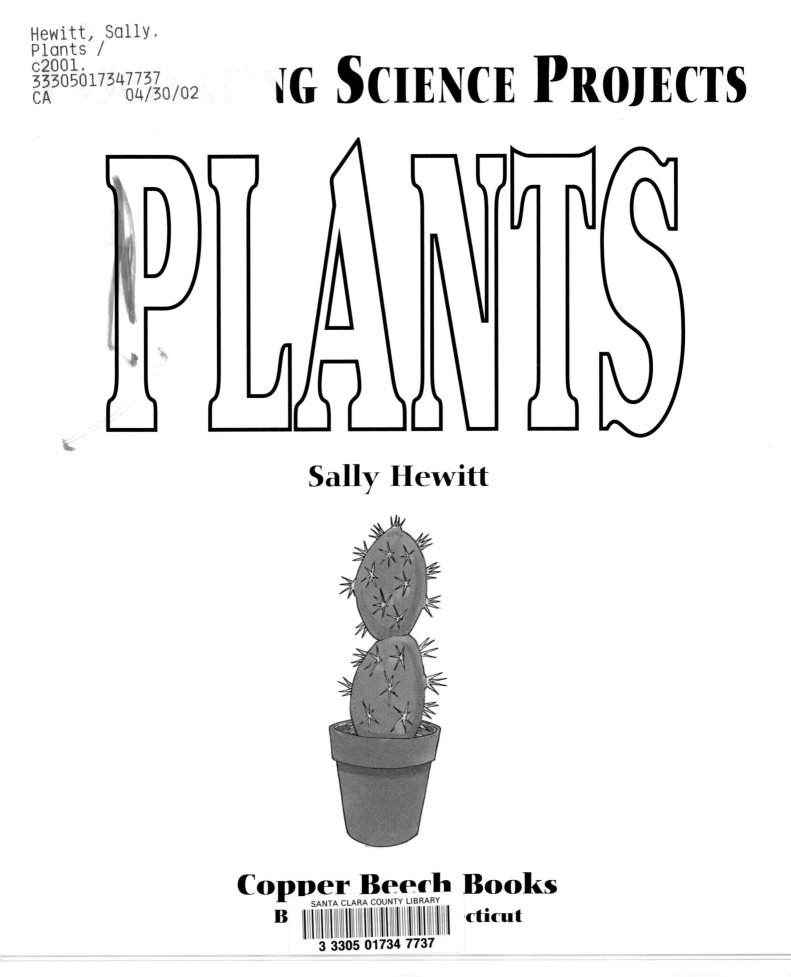

Copper Beech Books

B   cticut

© Aladdin Books Ltd 2001
Produced by
Aladdin Books Ltd
28 Percy Street
London W1P 0LD

ISBN 0–7613–2454–2 (lib. bdg.)
ISBN 0–7613–2283–3 (pbk.)

First published in the United States in 2001 by:
Copper Beech Books,
an imprint of
The Millbrook Press
2 Old New Milford Road
Brookfield, Connecticut 06804

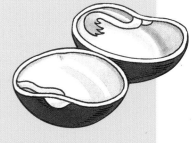

Designers:
Flick, Book design & graphics
Pete Bennett

Editor:
Sarah Milan

Illustrators:
Jim Eldridge, Andrew Geeson,
Catherine Ward, and Peter Wilks—SGA
Cartoons: Tony Kenyon—BL Kearley

Consultant:
Bryson Gore

Printed in Belgium

Cataloging-in-Publication Data is on file at the Library of Congress.

Contents

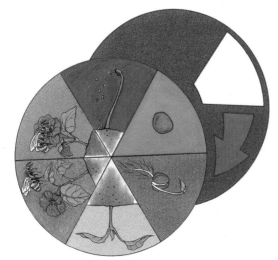

Introduction

In this book, the science of plants is explained through a series of fascinating projects and experiments. Each chapter deals with a different topic on plants, such as stems or flowers, and contains a major project that is fully supported by simple experiments, "Magic panels," and "Fascinating fact" boxes. At the end of every chapter is an explanation of what has happened and what this means. Projects requiring sharp tools or the use of heat or chemicals should be done with adult supervision.

This states the purpose of the project

METHOD NOTES
Helpful hints on things to remember when carrying out your project.

Materials
In this box is a full list of the items needed to carry out each main project.

1. The steps that describe how to carry out each project are listed clearly as numbered points.

2. Where there are illustrations to help you understand the instructions, the text refers to them as Figure 1, etc.

Figure 2

Figure 1

THE AMAZING MAGIC PANEL
This heading states what is happening

These boxes contain an activity or experiment that has a particularly dramatic or surprising result!

WHY IT WORKS
You can find out exactly what happened here, too.

WHAT THIS SHOWS

These boxes, which are headed either "What this shows" or "Why it works," contain an explanation of what happened during your project, why it happened, and the meaning of the result.

Fascinating facts!
An amusing or surprising fact related to the theme of the chapter.

The text in these circles links the theme of the topic from one page to the next in the chapter.

What is a plant?

Plants and every kind of animal, including human beings like you, are living things. All living things grow and make new life like themselves. Animals have babies, and new plants grow from seeds or bulbs and sometimes from roots, stems, or even leaves. Most animals move around because they have to search for food, but plants can stay rooted to one spot because they make their own food. Most plants use the green color in their leaves to make food from sunlight.

Explore the conditions plants need to grow

METHOD NOTES
It is best to use young, healthy plants for this experiment.

Materials
- five plants, e.g. geranium
- four plant pots
- a jam jar
- some soil
- a cardboard box
- petroleum jelly

1. Plant four of the plants in soil, each one in its own pot. Shake off the soil from the roots of the fifth plant.

2. Put the plants on a windowsill or somewhere with plenty of sunlight. Water the first plant (Figure 1) and watch it thrive and grow.

Figure 1

Figure 2

3. Don't water the second plant. Watch as the soil dries out and the leaves and stem begin to droop (Figure 2).

4. Cover the third plant with a box (Figure 3). Take off the box only to water the plant, so that it gets as little light as possible. Watch what begins to happen to the color of the leaves.

Figure 3

5. Water the fourth plant regularly, but spread some petroleum jelly all over both sides of some leaves (Figure 4). This will keep air from reaching them. Without air, watch as the leaves start to shrivel.

6. Put the fifth plant into a jar full of water (Figure 5). Can you see how the leaves are less green and the stem less strong than the first plant growing in soil?

Figure 4

Figure 5

WHAT THIS SHOWS

Plants need sunlight, air, water, and nutrients to grow. If a plant begins to look droopy, like the yucca below, it is not getting enough of at least one of these things.

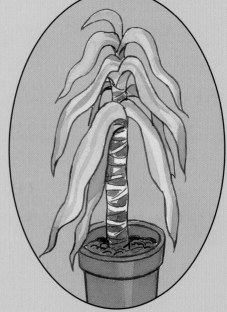

The plant with a good supply of water, sunlight, air, and soil will grow well. Like all living things, plants are made mainly of water, so they need a water supply. Without sunlight, plants cannot make food, so they grow weak and pale. And just like animals, plants need air to breathe. Plants benefit from plenty of nutrients (minerals) in the soil or water to help them grow healthy and strong.

7

What is a plant?

PARTS OF A PLANT

Most plants are flowering plants. But they can be as different as a huge chestnut tree and a tiny daisy. Nonflowering plants, such as ferns and seaweeds, have no flowers, but many have green leaves. Look closely at any flowering plant and you will find it has roots, a stem, leaves, and a flower.

A flower often has colorful petals to attract birds and insects. It contains all the parts needed to make a new plant. The stem supports the plant and carries water and minerals to the leaves and flowers. The green color in leaves is called chlorophyll. Sunlight is trapped in chlorophyll and turned into food for the plant. Roots hold the plant in place and suck up water and minerals from the soil.

flower

leaves

root

stem

Is it a pebble or a plant?
Stone plants are desert plants with juicy leaves. They have a clever way of hiding from hungry animals—they look just like pebbles! Their name, lithops, means "like a stone."

THE WHEEL OF LIFE

All living things go through a life cycle
—a new life begins and goes through
stages of growth to become an adult
that can start another new
life. Make a wheel of life
that goes around and
around to show the
life cycle of a
flowering plant.

Figure 1

Figure 2

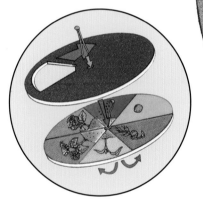

2. Cut
a window in
the other circle
and join the circles
together with a paper
clip (Figure 2). Turn the top circle
clockwise to reveal the life cycle.

1. Cut out two circles from cardboard.
Divide one circle into six parts and draw
six pictures showing these stages
(Figure 1): 1) Seed; 2) Seed sprouting
roots and shoots; 3) Young plant;
4) Bee leaving flower with pollen on
its legs; 5) Bee on another flower;
6) Seeds falling from dying flower.

Plants
are living things that need
certain conditions to grow. If they
have these, plants can make their
own food and can reproduce—
make new plants.

Roots

You can't usually see the roots of a plant because they grow underground. They spread downward and outward, holding the plant in place and sucking up water and minerals from the soil. Many plants, including most trees, have a main tap root with smaller roots growing out from it. Other plants have a mass of roots called diffuse roots. Each root has little root hairs and a cap on its tip that protects it as it pushes through the soil.

Discover what plants need to grow roots

Materials
- a geranium and an African violet
- three plant pots with soil
- two jars and a sharp knife
- rooting powder

METHOD NOTES
Use a sharp knife to cut the stems. A blunt knife will crush them.

1. Cut four stem tips from a plant such as a geranium. Strip the bottom leaves, leaving about an inch (3 cm) of stem.
2. Put the first stem in an empty jar (Figure 1).
3. Plant the second stem in a pot of soil and water it (Figure 2).
4. Put the third stem in a jar of water with no soil (Figure 3).

Figure 3

Figure 1

Figure 2

Figure 4

5. Dip the fourth stem in rooting powder, which encourages roots to grow, and plant it in soil (Figure 4).

6. Cut off the bottom of an African violet leaf and dip the cut edge in rooting powder. Push the cut edge into damp soil (Figure 5).

7. Look at the cuttings every day. Those whose leaves look healthy will have put down roots and will be growing into new plants. Can you see any of the growing roots?

Figure 5

WHAT THIS SHOWS

Plants will only put down roots when they are planted in the right conditions—they need water and sunlight or they will soon die. Plants are made up of cells, which are the smallest parts of any living thing.

In this experiment, the cells in the cuttings of the stems and leaves divide and make new cells, and roots start to grow. When plants make new plants like themselves this way, we call it vegetative reproduction. It can be a quick way of growing a new plant from an old one.

Monster roots!
Dandelions are unpopular with gardeners. They have a strong tap root that is very difficult to pull up as it can grow up to 15 inches (40 cm) long! If you leave a bit of the root behind when you are weeding, you can be sure that in time the dandelion will grow back again!

Some plants store sugars, starches, and fats to give them energy. Carrots are swollen roots and potatoes are swollen underground stems. Both store food for the growing plant.

Roots

GROW A NEW PLANT

You can grow a new plant from the top of root vegetables such as carrots and radishes. Slice off the top of a carrot and plant it in a saucer of soil. Water it, and in about two weeks leaves will start to sprout. If you have a backyard, plant it in the soil and see what happens. Can you see any tiny new roots?

THE AMAZING STARCH DETECTIVE
Detect starch in a potato

1. Buy a small bottle of iodine—a dark brown liquid used for treating cuts and bruises—from the pharmacist.
2. Get a potato and cut it in half.
3. Using a spoon, pour a drop of iodine onto the cut surface of the potato. You should see the potato turn bright blue.

WHY IT WORKS

Iodine reacts with starch by turning it blue, so you can tell from the blue patch that there is starch in the potato. This is because potatoes store starch as a source of energy.

See if you can also detect starch in another root vegetable, such as a carrot.

WATCH A PLANT SUCK IN WATER

You will need a potato, some sugar, a skewer, a see-through plastic drinking straw, a jar, and a spoon and pitcher for mixing.

1. Put a tablespoon of sugar and two tablespoons of water into the pitcher and stir until the sugar dissolves.

2. Use the skewer to bore a hole in the potato until it is the right size for the straw to fit tightly in.

3. Quarter fill the straw with the sugar solution.

4. Now put the potato in a jar of water. Watch as the solution rises gradually up inside the straw.

WHY IT WORKS

The solution expands and rises up inside the straw because of a process in plants called osmosis, by which water is absorbed into the plant (usually through the roots) to mix with its sugary sap. Water is drawn up into every part of the plant by osmosis.

Pull up some weeds and spread out their roots to see if they are bigger than the plant growing above the soil. You will probably need a spade to dig up weeds that have long roots like this dandelion.

Roots

hold a plant in place and suck up water and minerals from the soil. Sometimes they swell to store food. Stems and leaves can grow roots to make a new plant.

Stems

A stem does a similar job for a plant as a backbone does for you—it gives the plant support. It also contains tubes that transport essential water and minerals to the rest of the plant. Plants need sunlight to make their food, so another job for a stem is to reach for the light. A trunk is a strong, woody stem that allows a tree in a shady forest to grow very tall, up to the light. Other stems, like those of the ivy plant, curl and twist their way toward the Sun.

See how water travels up a stem

METHOD NOTES
This experiment works best with leafy celery and a pale-colored flower and leaf.

Materials
- a white carnation
- a stick of celery
- a leaf
- a sharp knife
- a pitcher of water
- three jars
- blue food coloring

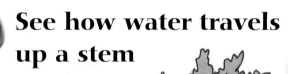

1. Cut a small piece from the end of the celery, the carnation, and the leaf stalk with a sharp knife. This will help them suck up the water.

2. Add the blue food coloring to the water to make a strong color. Pour some into each of the three jars.

Figure 1

14

Figure 2

Figure 3

3. Look carefully at all the parts of the celery stem, the carnation, and the leaf to see if you can find tubes like veins running through them.

4. Put the stick of celery into one of the jars of colored water (Figure 1) and put the carnation and the leaf into the other two jars.

5. After a few hours, the veins in the celery stalk and the leaf will turn blue (see Figure 3 for the leaf).

6. After a day, the tips of the flower petals will be blue. In three days, the whole flower will turn blue (Figure 2).

WHAT THIS SHOWS

After the roots have absorbed the water by osmosis, it is passed up the stem of the plant. In this experiment, you can see how the colored water makes its way up the stem, first into the leaves, then into the flowers. If you cut across the celery stalk after it has been in the blue water for a few hours, you will see little blue dots in the cut end. These are the tubes that carry water and minerals up the stem.

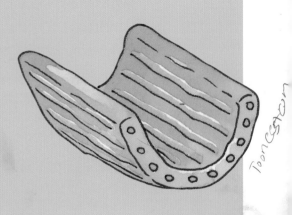

Stems

The tubes that carry water and minerals up the stem have strong walls that help keep the stem firm and hold the plant upright.

COMPARE FIRM AND WEAK STEMS
Woody stems are sturdy. Thinner, green stems need to be full of water to remain firm. Put a rose, a twig, and a green-stemmed flower such as a dandelion or tulip in a jar of water. Now put the same stems in an empty jar. In the jar without water, the woody stems will stay firm. But the green stems will droop, and so will the flowers and the leaves. Notice the differences between the stems in the two jars.

THE AMAZING PAPER FLOWERS
Show how capillary action works

1. Draw flower shapes on colored, but not shiny, paper. Stick a circle of a different color in the center.

2. Cut out your paper flowers carefully. Then curl each petal around a pencil, as shown. When you take the pencil out, each of the petals should stay curled up.

3. Put the flowers in water and watch the petals open out.

WHY IT WORKS
Paper is made of many fibers, and like a plant stem, is full of tiny tubes. Water clings to the sides of the tubes and rises up inside them. This is called capillary action. It fills the paper with water and opens out the petals. Water rises up the stem of a plant in the same way.

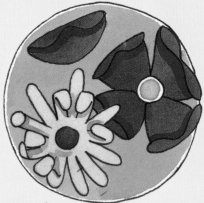

HOW STEMS GROW

Look at a plant or shrub (indoor or outdoor), and you will see that leaves and side stems grow out of the main stem. The bump from where they grow is called a node. The space between two nodes is called the internode. In the spring or summer, when the plant is growing, measure an internode between two nodes. You will find that however much the plant is growing, this length will stay about the same.

node

internode

WHAT THIS SHOWS
A branch or a stem grows from the tip. The part of the stem you measure may grow thicker, but it won't grow any longer. Look for leaf buds and new green leaves growing at the tip of stems and branches.

Tree acts like a sponge!
In Africa during the rainy season, the huge baobab tree stores precious water in its trunk, which swells with its extra load— up to 50 feet (15 m) in diameter! With the return of the dry season, the tree uses up the water, and its trunk shrinks again.

Stems
support a plant and carry water and minerals to every part of the plant. Some stems store water.

Leaves

The leaves of a plant are a particular shape and size so they can do their important job—manufacturing food—as efficiently as possible. Plants that grow in dark, shady places have big leaves to catch as much light as they can. In rainy climates, leaves often have a shiny, waterproof coat. Some leaves have prickles to protect them and others are tough to survive the cold.

Learn why some plants sweat

Materials
- a potted plant
- a cactus in a pot
- two clear plastic bags

METHOD NOTES
Make sure both plants have been watered recently.

1. Choose a houseplant, such as a begonia, that has plenty of leaves and cover it completely with a clear plastic bag, making sure no air can escape (Figure 1).
2. Cover the cactus in exactly the same way. Be very careful of the prickles.
3. Put both plants in a warm, sunny place.

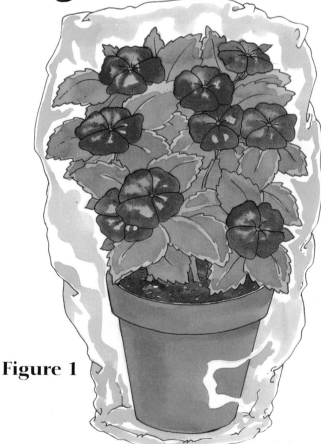

Figure 1

The prickles are the cactus' leaves

Swollen stem of cactus

WHAT THIS SHOWS

The houseplant leaves lose moisture in a process called transpiration—the term for the flow of water through a plant. Tiny root hairs suck up water from the soil into the roots. The water then climbs the narrow tubes in the stem and goes into the leaves.

underside of leaf

stomata

Plants breathe through tiny holes called stomata on the underside of the leaves. As water escapes through these holes and out into the air, more water is pulled up through the plant.

The green part of a cactus is a swollen stem. Its leaves have become prickles that have no stomata, so the cactus loses as little water as possible in the dry desert where it grows.

4. After several hours, look at the bags. Rub them both with your fingers. There will be drops of water on the inside of the bag covering the houseplant. The bag covering the cactus will be dry inside. The houseplant seems to have been sweating, but not the cactus.

Leaves

COMPARE DIFFERENT LEAVES

Collect as many different leaves as you can—deciduous, evergreen, simple, and compound. A leaf with one blade—the flat, green part—is a simple leaf. A compound leaf, such as a horse chestnut leaf, is made up of several blades. Pine needles are very thin leaves with a tough wax coating that can survive cold winters.

Deciduous trees have big green leaves that collect sunlight in spring and summer. In the fall when it gets colder, the leaves fall and die. Evergreen trees keep their leaves all year round.

holly

pine

horse chestnut

laurel

oak

maple

Put the leaves in a shoe box and shut the lid. Check them every few days. Do all the leaves dry out and crumble? Do any become "skeleton" leaves, when all that is left is the veins? Do the evergreen leaves survive the longest?

Try making some leaf rubbings. Lay white paper over a leaf with its underside facing up. Rub the paper evenly with a wax crayon and see the leaf shape and its raised pattern of veins appear.

Treetop swimming pool!
Bromeliads grow on the top branches of rain forest trees to get near the sunlight, but their roots can't reach the ground. So their huge leaves catch raindrops to create pools high up in the tree!

FALL COLORS

In late summer, find a deciduous tree with green leaves that will change color in the fall. Choose a leaf growing in bright sunlight. Cover half of it with tin foil (Figure 1), but don't remove it from the tree. In fall, when the leaves have changed color, take off the foil (Figure 2).

Figure 1

Figure 2

WHAT THIS SHOWS

In fall, leaves lose their green chlorophyll, and other colors—reds and golds—show through. The part of the leaf covered in foil was not getting any sunlight. This made it lose its chlorophyll and become paler.

Plants lose water through their leaves in a process called transpiration. Leaves use sunlight to make food for the plant.

Sunlight

If you miss a meal or haven't had enough to drink, you soon start to feel hungry and thirsty, and probably quite tired. Like you, plants need food and water or they will wilt and die. Because plants cannot move around, they need to grow in a place where they can get sunlight, water, and air. If a plant is growing in a dark, shady place, it will work very hard to grow toward the Sun because without sunlight, a plant cannot make food.

Make a potato maze to see how plants grow toward light

METHOD NOTES
Find a potato with "eyes" or buds from which a shoot will grow.

Materials
- a shoe box
- a lid
- some cardboard
  - roll of tape
  - scissors
  - a potato

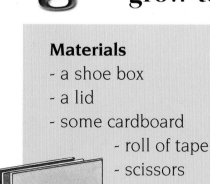

Figure 1

1. Make a small hole in one end of the shoe box, just big enough to let in a little light (Figure 1). Cut three strips of cardboard a bit shorter than the width of the box.

Figure 2

2. Bend back one end of each strip to make a flap. Tape the straps to the side of the box as in Figure 2.

3. Put the potato at the other end of the box from the hole you have cut, and put on the lid. Place the box in a well-lit, airy position.

Figure 3

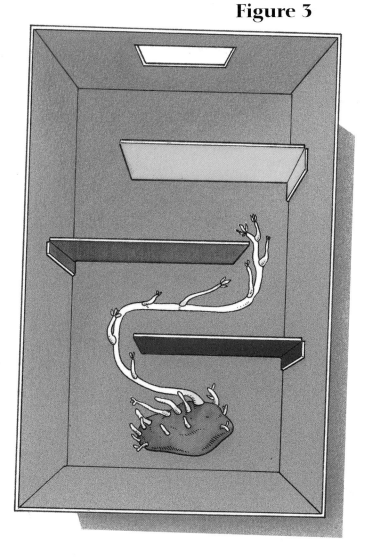

4. The potato is full of stored food that the new plant needs to grow, so after a few days, it will start a shoot. The shoot will bend its way through the maze toward the light (Figure 3).

WHAT THIS SHOWS

If you put a potato in a maze, as you have done in this experiment, or if you plant a bean upside down in soil (see below), the shoots will always find their way toward the light, even if it means they have to wind their way around other things. Sunlight is essential for a plant's survival. This is because plants use sunlight to make food in a process called photosynthesis.

Green leaves use energy from the Sun to make food from water and from a gas in the air called carbon dioxide. The food, called glucose, is carried through tubes to the rest of the plant. In the final stage of photosynthesis, oxygen, the gas that we and other animals breathe in, is given out into the air.

Plants use sunlight to make food for themselves through photosynthesis. The word photosynthesis means "putting together with light." Plants also need sunlight to provide them with warmth.

Sunlight

MAKE A MINI-GREENHOUSE

When plants are grown in a greenhouse, they are protected from the cold, but are exposed to the maximum amount of sunlight. Gardeners grow seedlings under glass for this reason. And plants from hot climates will grow in cold climates as long as they are in a greenhouse. Sow some grass seed in a seed tray and leave it in a sunny place outside. Cover some of the seeds with a glass jar. Watch how much faster the seedlings grow under glass.

Flies for supper!
A Venus flytrap grows in poor soil where there are no gardeners to fertilize it. To add to its diet, it traps and eats any fly foolish enough to land on one of its leaves.

WHY IT WORKS

Sunlight shines through the glass and heats the air trapped inside. The grass seedlings will grow much faster in the warmer air under the glass than the seedlings in the colder air.

THE AMAZING BUBBLING LEAVES
Watch leaves produce bubbles in water

Put some fresh green leaves in a bowl of water and leave them in the sunlight. Can you see bubbles coming from them? You may need to look through a magnifying glass.

WHY IT WORKS

During photosynthesis, plants give out oxygen, the gas that we need to breathe, into the air. The leaves you have put in water photosynthesize in the sunlight, sending out bubbles of oxygen that are visible in the water. In the same way, water plants help keep ponds and rivers full of the oxygen that fish and other water creatures need to breathe.

MAKE LEAF STENCILS

Choose a houseplant with big green leaves, such as a rubber plant.
Cut out some cardboard shapes smaller than the leaves. With poster putty, stick the shapes on some of the leaves that face the sunlight. After about a week, take off the shapes. The leaf underneath has turned pale because without light, green chlorophyll breaks down faster than the plant replaces it.

Plants need sunlight to make their own food, and shoots will always find their way toward the light. Oxygen is given out during photosynthesis.

Flowers

Next time you pass a flowerbed with colorful scented flowers, stop and look inside one of the flowers. In its center, you will find a yellowy-orange powder called pollen. Color and scent act like an advertisement. They tell insects, birds, and sometimes small animals that this is where they can find a sweet liquid called nectar to drink. While they are drinking, the pollen sticks to their legs and bodies, and they carry it from flower to flower, pollinating as they go.

Identify parts of a flower

Materials
- a flower (see Method notes)
- pieces of cardboard
- pens and pencils
- clear tape
- a magnifying glass
- tweezers

1. Notice the scent and color of the petals on your flower. Do they have a pattern leading to the center of the flower? (This is a "honey guide" and leads insects toward the nectar in the center.)

METHOD NOTES
A lily, a tulip, or a buttercup are all good flowers to choose for this activity.

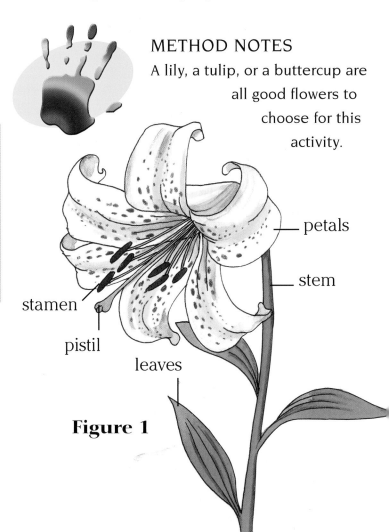

petals

stem

stamen

pistil

leaves

Figure 1

26

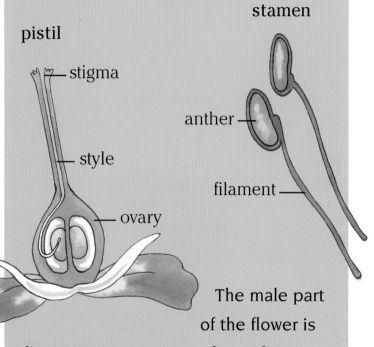

Figure 2

2. Pull off the petals and count them.

3. Pull off and count the delicate stamens (see Figure 1).

4. Now find the pistil and gently cut it from the flower. Find the sticky stigma, the style, and the ovary inside the pistil. These are shown in the box on the right.

5. Mount all the pieces onto cardboard and label each of the parts (Figure 2).

Grass flowers are small and dull with no scent because they don't have to attract insects. Their pollen is carried from flower to flower by the wind.

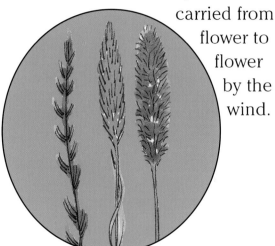

WHAT THIS SHOWS

The pistil and stamens that you have removed are the parts of the flower that make seeds from which new plants can grow. The female part of the flower is the pistil, which is made up of a sticky stigma, the style, and the ovary, where seeds are formed.

stamen

pistil

stigma

anther

style

filament

ovary

The male part of the flower is the stamen. At its tip is the anther, where the pollen is made. Insects carry pollen from the anther of one flower to the stigma of another. When a grain of pollen sticks to the stigma, a pollen tube grows down into the ovary. The pollen grain travels down the tube and into the ovary. Then seeds start to form.

Flowers

DRAWING FLOWERS ON CARDBOARD

You will find flowers growing in yards and parks and growing wild in the countryside. Take a sketchbook, a pencil, and colored crayons and make detailed drawings of the flowers you see. Then look up the flowers in a field guide.

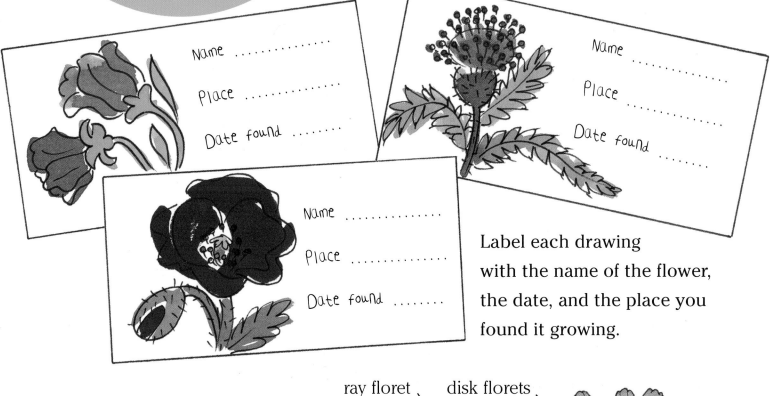

Name ....

Place ....

Date found ....

Name ....

Place ....

Date found ....

Name ....

Place ....

Date found ....

Label each drawing with the name of the flower, the date, and the place you found it growing.

FLOWER HEADS

Daisies are not just one flower, but lots of tiny flowers all clustered together on one flower head. Each petal is a little flower called a ray floret. The flowers in the center, which are often yellow, are disk florets.

ray floret   disk florets

MAKE SOME POTPOURRI

You can fill your room with the scent of roses even after the roses have died. Hang a bunch of roses upside down in a warm, dry place. When the flowers have dried out, shake the petals into a bowl. This is called potpourri. Move the petals around gently to release their delicate perfume.

What a stink!
The giant rafflesia is not only the biggest and heaviest flower in the world, it is also one of the smelliest. It depends on meat-eating flies to pollinate it. To attract the flies, it produces the terrible smell of rotten meat!

VISITORS

Sit quietly and watch creatures visiting flowers. As well as bees, you may see butterflies—they drink nectar from many flowers. Notice how some flowers smell sweeter at night. This is to attract moths.

Flowers
are usually brightly colored and scented to attract the birds, insects, and other creatures that pollinate them. They have all the parts needed to make seeds so a new plant can grow.

Fruit and seeds

Once a flower has completed its job and the petals have died, the ovary becomes the fruit that contains the seeds. Some fruits, like apples and peaches, are juicy and good to eat. Others, like poppy fruits, are dry pods full of little black seeds. Sometimes we eat the seeds as well as the fruit: strawberries, for example, are covered in little seeds. Blackberries, maple wings, and dandelion parachutes are all very different-looking fruits containing seeds.

Match fruits with their seeds

METHOD NOTES
After you have cut open the fruit, make it into a fruit salad and eat it!

Materials
- a knife
- a chopping board
- a selection of fruit

1. Cut open different kinds of fruit and look for the seeds inside. (It's easy to tell a fruit from a vegetable. Most fruits contains seeds, and most vegetables do not.)
2. Separate the seeds from the fruits and put them in two piles. Can you remember which seed belonged to which fruit?
3. You can try planting the seeds. Some might grow into new plants.

GROW AN AVOCADO

You can grow a new plant from an avocado seed. Push four toothpicks firmly into the seed and balance it on top of a jar of water with the large end pointing down. Keep checking to make sure the water just covers the base of the seed. Within a few weeks, roots will begin to grow down and a shoot will push up through the seed.

WHAT THIS SHOWS

The fruit is the part of the plant that contains the seeds. Many fruits are juicy, sweet-smelling, or shiny to tempt animals to eat them—look at the fruits you have cut open and the avocado. Animals and birds eat the fruit, often swallowing the seeds whole. The seeds fall to the ground in their droppings and find a new place to grow.

Giant seed braves rough seas!
A coconut is the enormous seed of a coconut palm. Palm trees grow on the seashore, and when coconuts fall into the water, they float out to sea. Sometimes they float thousands of miles before they drift onto another beach and grow into a new palm tree!

Fruit and seeds

There are all kinds of dangers waiting for newly formed seeds. Plants have to produce a huge number of them because only a few will find a good place to grow.

COMPARE WAYS THAT SEEDS DISPERSE

If seeds landed closely around the plant they came from, they would all be competing for the same soil, water, and light. For the best chance of survival, they need to disperse—spread out as widely as possible. Collect some fruit and seeds in the fall and look at how they disperse.

Maple seeds whirl away on wings.

Dandelion parachutes catch the wind.

Holly berry seeds fall to the ground in birds' droppings.

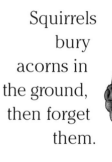

Squirrels bury acorns in the ground, then forget them.

Burdock hooks catch onto the coats of passing animals.

THE AMAZING POPPING CORN
Show the effect of heat on popcorn seeds

Ask an adult to help!
Warm a teaspoon of vegetable oil in a large pan. Add 4 ounces (100 g) of popcorn and put on a tight-fitting lid. Hear the corn popping inside. When the popping stops, carefully take off the lid to find lots of fluffy popcorn.

WHY IT WORKS
Un-popped popcorn grains are small, yellow seeds with tough skins and starchy insides. The heat causes the starch to expand so much that eventually the skin bursts with a pop! Now you can add salt or sugar to the popcorn and eat it.

MYSTERY SEEDS

Gardeners sow seeds they want to grow in their garden and pull up weeds from seeds that have planted themselves. Find out which seeds have found their way into the soil and are waiting to grow.

1. Dig up some soil from two different places—a shady place under a tree and a sunny place by a wall.

2. Put each soil sample in its own seed tray and label where the soil came from. Water both trays regularly.

3. Soon, even though you didn't plant any seeds, shoots will start to grow from seeds already in the soil.

You may see more shoots growing in the soil under the tree because birds and animals drop seeds as they sit in the tree.

Watch for seeds growing in places that you would never imagine they could reach. Can you find shoots growing through cracks in the sidewalk or even halfway up a wall?

We have seen that fruit and seeds are often good to eat and that plants have different ways of making sure that their seeds have the best chance of finding somewhere to grow.

Waiting to grow

In parts of the world that have four seasons—spring, summer, fall, and winter—many plants have a life cycle that takes a year to complete. Seeds germinate (grow a root and a shoot) in spring when the weather is getting warm. Flowers blossom in summer, when there are plenty of insects around to pollinate them. Fruit and seeds form in the fall, when animals are fattening themselves up for winter. Seeds and bulbs wait in the soil over winter before they germinate again in the spring.

Watch a seed grow a root and shoot

METHOD NOTES
Buy a seed packet of white beans. They will be dry and hard.

Materials
- a packet of white beans
- a paper towel
- a jam jar
- a pitcher of water
- a plate

2. Crumple a paper towel and put it into a clean glass jam jar. Carefully push at least two beans between the towel and the side of the jar (Figure 2).

1. Soak the beans overnight to soften their tough seed coat (Figure 1).

Figure 1

Figure 2

3. Sprinkle water onto the towel and make sure you keep it damp throughout this experiment.

4. Leave the jar in a warm, dark place, as the beans would be if they were in soil. After about a week, the beans should start to germinate.

5. Bring the jar out into the light and watch the beans grow into bean plants (Figure 3). As the bean plants get taller, try planting them in soil. One day you might be able to harvest beans from your plant.

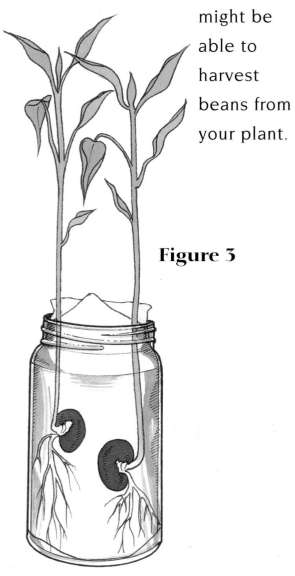

Figure 3

WHY IT WORKS

Inside the seed is the embryo—the root and shoot that will grow into the new plant. The pale, fleshy part of the bean is the food store, which the young plant will need until it grows leaves and can start to make its own food. Outside is the tough skin that protects the bean.

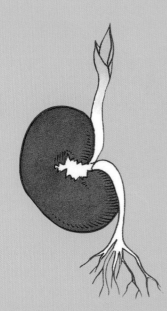

Dry seeds will not start to grow in their seed packets. The seeds need three things to germinate—warmth, water to swell the seed, and oxygen. Once they have these, most seeds will germinate and grow into a new plant.

Waiting to grow

LOOK AT CONDITIONS FOR GERMINATION

Find four trays and fill one with soil, one with water, one with pebbles, and leave one empty. Sprinkle them all with mustard seeds. Put the trays in a light airy place. Water them all except the seeds in the empty tray. Which seeds have air, water, and warmth to germinate and which grow into a new plant?

Put a tray of seeds in soil in the refrigerator and one near a heating vent to find out the effect of temperature on germination.

Beautiful desert carpet!
Seeds lie dormant in the desert sand, where it may not rain for years. When at last the rain comes, the seeds spring to life, and the desert is suddenly carpeted with brightly colored flowers!

SPROUTING VEGETABLES

An onion is a bulb and a potato is a swollen stem called a tuber. They are both parts of a plant from which a new plant can grow. Find an onion and a potato that have been forgotten at the bottom of the vegetable rack. Have they grown shoots and roots? Are they shriveling as the growing plant uses up its stored food?

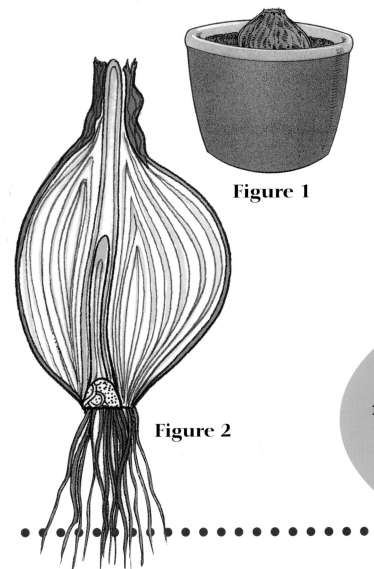

Figure 1

Figure 2

SPRING BULBS

In the fall, plant a daffodil, tulip, or hyacinth bulb in a pot and leave it in a cold, dark place (Figure 1). Bring it out and water it in the early spring. The warmth will wake it up and it will start to grow. If you cut through a bulb, you will see layers of thickened leaves storing food (Figure 2).

We have discovered that inside seeds or bulbs are the embryos of new plants. Seeds and bulbs will lie dormant until the conditions are right for them to start to grow (see pages 6–7).

Cycle of matter

In nature, dead plants are not wasted. They rot back into the soil and help to make it rich and full of nutrients for new plants to grow in. Gardeners often pile up leaves, grass clippings, and dead plants to make a compost pile. Once the garden trash is properly rotted, it can be dug into the soil as a home-made fertilizer. But not all trash is good for the soil. Some takes a very long time to rot, and may pollute the soil.

Compare how well different trash rots

METHOD NOTES
Don't open the bags after the trash has started to rot.

Materials
- three clear plastic bags
- household gloves
- garbage, such as stale bread
- some leaves, twigs and flowers
- manufactured trash
- a trowel
- a pitcher of water

1. Wearing gloves and using a trowel, put some soil into three clear plastic bags. Add some water.

2. Put some leaves, dead flowers, and twigs in the first bag (Figure 1). In the second bag, put some manufactured trash—such as plastic bottles, soda cans, and milk cartons (Figure 2). Put an apple core,

Figure 2

Figure 1

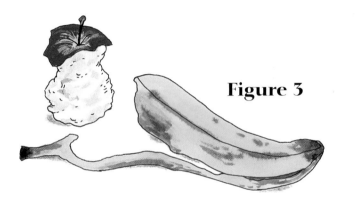

Figure 3

a banana peel, and some bread in the third bag (Figure 3).

3. Shake the bags to mix the trash in with the soil and water, and then seal each bag. Check them every few days to see what happens to the trash.

Of the natural things, the banana skin and twigs will take longest to rot. Of the manufactured things, nothing will rot unless it is made of biodegradable plastic, and even then it will take a long time.

WHY IT WORKS

Wood, leaves, and dead plants are all biodegradable, natural materials. Anything that is biodegradable can be broken down by living things called decomposers. These might be tiny microbes, insects, worms, or fungi.

Mushrooms, toadstools, yeasts, and molds are all kinds of fungi that feed on plants and animals. If you see fungi growing on a fallen tree trunk, you know it will be helping to break down the dead wood.

Manufactured materials such as plastic are nonbiodegradable. Scientists are still trying to discover new materials that will rot naturally and not cause pollution.

Cycle of matter

Soil may look like brown mud, but if you examine it closely, you will see it is a mixture of tiny pieces of rock, stones, twigs, and decaying plants and animals.

SEE HOW SOIL BREAKS DOWN

The weather gradually wears down rock into tiny particles, which gather together until there is enough soil for small plants to grow. Soil may be made of large grains of sand, or small particles of chalk or clay, depending on the kind of rock that formed it. You can examine the different types of rock particles that make up the soil near you.

Figure 1

You will need a trowel, a strainer, a bucket, a big glass jar with a lid, and a magnifying glass.

1. Dig up some soil and strain it into the bucket (Figure 1). Examine the large bits left behind in the strainer.

Figure 3

Figure 2

2. Put some strained earth in the jar, add some water, screw on the lid, and give it a good shake (Figure 2).
3. Let the earth settle into layers then look at them closely with the magnifying glass (Figure 3). Can you see the larger particles at the bottom and the smaller ones near the top?

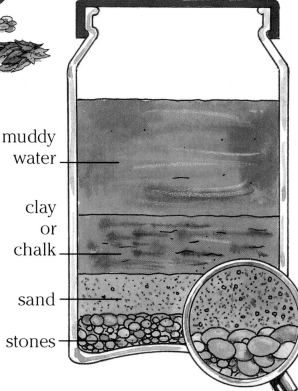

muddy water

clay or chalk

sand

stones

40

1. Choose a mushroom with dark gills under its smooth, pale cap.
2. Pull off its stalk and place the cap, gill side down, on some white paper. Cover it with a bowl and leave it overnight.
3. The next day, remove the bowl and carefully lift the mushroom.

You will see a beautiful dark brown print where the spores have fallen from the gills onto the paper.
WHY IT WORKS
Mushrooms, like all fungi, don't grow from seeds. They produce tiny cells called spores in their gills, from which new mushrooms grow.

MOLDY BREAD AND FRUIT

Fruit and bread that are left lying around for too long soon get moldy. Sprinkle an orange and a slice of white bread with water, seal them both in clear plastic bags, and leave them in a warm place. The orange will start to shrivel and they will both turn blue-green with mold.

WHY IT WORKS

Mold is a kind of plant that helps things rot. Like a mushroom, it spreads with spores. Mold spores are always in the air around us, so don't open the bags and let out more spores! When you have finished, throw them away still sealed.

Plants break down and return to the soil, making it rich for new plants to grow. Fungi and mold help that rotting process. Nothing is wasted in nature.

Plants for life

Every living thing needs energy to live and grow. That is why the Sun is so important for life on Earth. Plants make their own food using energy from the Sun, and other living things eat either plants or plant-eating animals. Plants are called producers because they make or produce their own food. All animals are called consumers because they eat or consume food that they haven't made for themselves. This means that without plants, no animal could live.

Make a web of life

Materials
- cardboard
- scissors
- a hole punch
- green and red yarn
- colored pens
- tape

Figure 1

1. Cut small rectangles of cardboard and fold under one end to make a stand (Figure 1). Punch one hole in the top of each piece.

METHOD NOTES
It is best to choose animals that live in the same habitat for your web of life.

2. Cut out animal pictures or draw them onto the cardboard. Draw or paste a plant picture onto one of the pieces (Figure 2).

3. Link all the herbivores (plant-eating animals) to the plant card with green yarn. Use tape to hold the yarn in place.

4. Now link the carnivores (meat-eating

Figure 2

animals) to the herbivores they eat with red yarn. Some animal cards will have more than one piece of red yarn attached to them.

5. Stand all the cards up, and trace the link from each animal back to the plant card. If you pick up any one card, the others will all go up with it since they are all linked in a web of life.

WHAT THIS SHOWS

All animals, whether herbivores or carnivores, depend on plants or plant matter for food. With no plants, there would be no herbivores, and with no herbivores, there would be no carnivores or omnivores (animals that eat plants and other animals). The name we give to a place where plants and animals live and grow together is a habitat. You could make a web of life for the plants and animals in any habitat and find that they are all linked in a similar way to the plants and animals shown above.

Plants for life

Humans are omnivores, which means we can eat both plants and animals. People who are vegetarians choose to eat only plants and no meat.

EDIBLE PARTS OF A PLANT

Human beings have learned to grow plants that are good to eat. We have also learned which parts of a plant are tastiest. Next time you eat vegetables or fruit, think about which part of the plant you are eating.

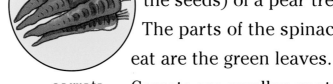

carrots (roots)

Pears are the juicy fruit (containing the seeds) of a pear tree.

The parts of the spinach plant we eat are the green leaves.

Carrots are swollen roots storing starch and sugar for the plant.

Broccoli is clusters of tiny flowers.

The center of a sunflower is packed with seeds that can be pressed to make sunflower oil.

Asparagus spears are tender stems.

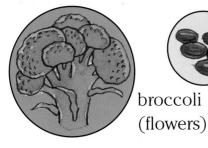

pears (fruit)

spinach (leaves)

sunflower (seeds)

broccoli (flowers)

asparagus (stems)

DISCOVER WHAT LIVES IN A TREE

A tree creates a habitat for all kinds of creatures. Choose a tree with a low branch and lay a big piece of paper underneath it. Shake the branch and examine the bugs and creepy-crawlies that land on your paper.

Rain forest riches!
More than half of all the
kinds of plants in the world grow in rain
forests. More than 2,000 kinds can
grow in a single square block! This is
why rain forests are so precious.

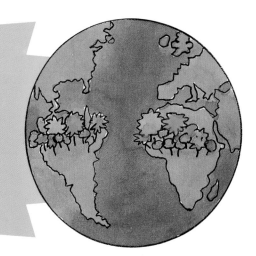

Try creating a
pond with pond
weed to attract
water creatures.
Or leave a patch
of nettles in your
backyard for
caterpillars
to eat.

PLANT A WINDOW BOX

If you live in a city where few plants
grow, there probably won't be very
many animals or insects either.
Plant a window box with sweet-
smelling flowers and herbs, and
butterflies and bees will come
looking for nectar.

We
have seen how life depends
on plants, and how all living things
are linked together in a web of life.
With no plants, there would be no
habitats for other creatures.

Glossary

biodegradable

Biodegradable materials are broken down naturally when decomposers get to work on them. Decomposers are living things such as insects, worms, fungi, or tiny microbes. Wood and dead plants are biodegradable natural materials that rot back into the soil.

capillary action

Capillary action is the way liquid goes along narrow tubes called capillaries. The liquid clings to the sides of the tube and is drawn along it. Water rises up the tubes in the stem of a plant by capillary action.

chlorophyll

Chlorophyll is the green color plants use to trap light energy from the Sun to make their own food. Without light, plants cannot make chlorophyll and they lose their green color.

deciduous

Deciduous trees lose their leaves in the fall. This helps them to save energy in the winter when there is less daylight and water for them to make food in their leaves. During the winter, their growth slows down, and they live off food they stored during the summer.

embryo

An embryo is a living thing in the early stages of its development. A plant embryo inside a seed such as a bean will grow into an adult plant with roots, a stem, leaves, and flowers.

evergreen

Evergreen trees are always green. They keep their leaves all year round, growing new leaves before shedding the old ones. Their leaves often have a tough, leathery coat to protect them from cold weather during the winter.

osmosis

Osmosis is the way water moves across a very thin skin called a membrane to mix with a solution such as sugar and water. Water is sucked from the soil into the roots of a plant by osmosis.

photosynthesis

Photosynthesis is the way plants make food. They use a gas in the air called carbon dioxide, water, and energy from sunlight to make food in chlorophyll—the green color in their leaves. During this process, they give out oxygen.

pollination

Pollination is the way pollen is carried by birds or insects or by the wind from one flower to another. Pollen made in the male part—the anther—of one flower is transferred to the female part—the stigma—of another flower.

seed dispersal

Seed dispersal is the way the seeds of a plant are scattered. They can be dispersed by the wind, by animals, or they can whirl away on wings.

stomata

Stomata are the tiny holes on the underside of a leaf that allow a plant to breathe. They open to let carbon dioxide in and oxygen out during photosynthesis.

transpiration

Transpiration is the way plants lose water through their leaves. It escapes as a gas called water vapor through the stomata.

vegetative reproduction

Vegetative reproduction is the way a plant can make another plant like itself from a part of itself such as a bulb or a cutting.

Index

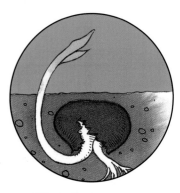

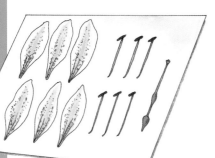